A VICTORIAN TABLE

PHOTOGRAPHY AND DESIGN
BY KOREN TRYGG
TEXT BY LUCY POSHEK

ANTIOCH GOURMET
GIFT BOOKS

Published by Antioch Publishing Company
Yellow Springs, Ohio 45387

Copyright © 1993 Antioch Publishing Company
Photography and Design © 1993 Koren Trygg
Text © 1993 Lucy Poshek

ISBN 0-89954-826-1

A VICTORIAN TABLE

Printed and bound in the U.S.A.

CONTENTS

VICTORIAN DINING TRADITIONS

At few other times has dining reached such heights of elegance and civility than during Queen Victoria's reign, from 1837 to 1901. Indeed, nineteenth-century writer Oscar Wilde might not have been exaggerating when he said, "A man who can dominate a London dinner table can dominate the world."

When Victoria ascended the throne, tremendous changes were evolving in British, European and American society. The rise of industry had created economic growth and a new middle class with increased wealth. Also, the arrival of the railroad and faster ships shortened travel time between countries, ending their cultural isolation. It was an age of powerful progress.

The nineteenth century was also an era of rigorous social climbing. The newly well-to-do wasted no time in seeking ways to display their wealth and emulate the upper classes. What better avenue than at social occasions? Consequently, a greater amount of attention was lavished on entertaining, and the dining room became the social center of every aspiring household. A beautifully set table, abundance of food and servants, and genteel manners all grew to epic levels of importance.

In the early Victorian period, most middle to upper class family dinners consisted of two or three courses with several dishes at each course. At a dinner party, it was not uncommon to have at least five courses with as many

as twenty-five different dishes. As the century passed, however, the number of dishes within each course were reduced, resulting in less lengthy meals.

The style of serving meals also changed by the end of the Victorian period. Under the old English method, every dish for each course was placed on the table at once. The goal was to impress one's guests by filling every space on the table. Under the new service *à la Russe*, the dishes for each course were placed on a sideboard so that servants could hand them around to guests in rotation. Service *à la Russe* not only eased the burden of trying to serve many dishes simultaneously, but also opened up the table for decoration.

Although the number of dishes and serving methods were gradually simplified, Victorian food remained sumptuous by today's standards. This was largely because meat, fowl, game, and dairy products were all abundant and affordable during the nineteenth century. For instance, oysters and salmon—now considered expensive delicacies—were used liberally in cooking even among the poor. Not only was the land rich and waters plentiful, but the railroad made it possible to transport fresh produce more quickly.

Improved transportation also brought new foreign influences to British and American cooking. The French chef, Auguste Escoffier, was the most respected culinary authority of the time. French cuisine became so fashionable among the upper classes that most dinner menus were printed strictly in French.

In Britain, India was another foreign influence that

affected Victorian cookery. The British colonials brought back many favorite recipes from India, including chutney (a relish often served with cold meats) and curry dishes.

The working population, however, preferred simple, regional dishes that emphasized local products. Each region of Britain had delightful names for these dishes— Singin' Hinnies, Yorkshire Fat Rascals, Hindle Wakes, and Huckle-my-Buff, to name a few. And, after Queen Victoria and her beloved Prince Albert acquired their Highland castle in the 1840's, many regional Scottish dishes, such as Cock-a-Leekie and Glasgow Magistrates, became equally popular.

Victorians of all classes had traditional meals for every special event, including Hallowe'en, The Harvest Festival, Thanksgiving, All Souls, Shrove Tuesday, Easter, Fourth of July, Guy Fawkes, Burns' Night, and St. Patrick's Day. And nothing rivaled the festive bounty and holiday splendor of a Victorian Christmas.

As the dining room became the focus of Victorian social life and the quest for gentility grew, a more structured set of table rituals developed. Good table manners were, after all, the first sign of a lady or gentleman's social position. In response to a growing demand for guidance, a host of new etiquette books appeared during this time. One of the most widely read was Isabella Beeton's *Book of Household Management*, published in 1861. Presenting a thorough guide to Victorian manners and eating habits, Mrs. Beeton defined dining as "the privilege of civilization. The nation which knows how to dine has learnt the leading lesson of progress."

Today, some Victorian table and cooking rituals are undeniably outmoded. Many nineteenth-century recipes are too rich and elaborate to reproduce now, and we no longer have a household of servants to help prepare dishes the old-fashioned way.

But Queen Victoria's 63-year reign came to represent the peak of dining splendor largely because the Victorians took joy in rituals and extra little touches at the table. They entertained with many charming customs which we can still use in our own modern-day lives—customs which will not only keep our family heritage alive but also give our homes an extra touch of graciousness and caring.

In this hectic world it would benefit us to rekindle a few Victorian dining rituals such as a heartwarming breakfast, a soothing afternoon tea, and an elegant dinner table. We can create new traditions of our own by turning to the past and observing the useable, distinctive details of the Victorian table.

"But a big dinner, with a hired chef and two borrowed footmen, with Roman punch, roses from Henderson's, and menus on gilt-edged cards, was a different affair, and not to be lightly undertaken. As Mrs. Archer remarked, the Roman punch made all the difference; not in itself but by its manifold implications— since it signified either canvas-backs or terrapin, two soups, a hot and a cold sweet, full décolletage with short sleeves, and guests of a proportionate importance."
EDITH WHARTON

VICTORIAN TABLE TOUCHES

"There is no pleasanter sight than an artistically set dinner table just before the guests are seated," wrote the author of *How to Behave and How to Amuse*, in 1890. Besides manners, cuisine and hospitality, a beautifully set table was regarded as the crown of Victorian refinement. Many hours were spent on the table decorations. Hostesses even drew up detailed plans in advance, showing the position of every item on the table. Today, however, our goal is to reproduce some of those Victorian table touches without exhausting our energies or pocketbooks.

The Victorians had a passion for luxurious table linens and trims of lace, ribbons, fringe, braids, and tassels. White damask, lace or crocheted tablecloths were usually used, but in their absence a plain white cloth would do. Add a touch of romance by gathering the skirt of the tablecloth with a graceful ribbon tied at either end. In lieu of a tablecloth, place a lace runner down the center of the table (good for setting off the centerpiece) with lace doilies serving as placemats.

Victorian napkins were large, starched, and sometimes folded into intricate shapes. Although napkin rings were often used, you could instead tie each napkin with a ribbon and perhaps tuck in a single flower. Because the Victorians adored nature, a profusion of indoor plants and

flowers were found in every household. During the 1870's and 80's, flowers on the table were at their most lavish. Ivy—often woven among the candleholders—and roses were particular favorites. The tiered centerpieces, or epergnes, as they were called then, usually contained fresh flowers or fruit. Sometimes individual bouquets for the ladies were placed in little vases while boutonnieres for the gentlemen were found in the folds of their napkins.

The Victorians wielded many table utensils that included now-obsolete items such as corn cob scrapers, angel food cake breakers, nut and olive picks, asparagus tongs, and aspic slicers. But one refreshing custom which will delight your guests is the Victorian ritual of finger bowls. Float a slice of lemon, fragrant sprig of herbs, or flowers in small bowls of water and bring them out before dessert.

Another elegant custom at Victorian dinner parties was the use of place cards. Write out the names of your guests in calligraphy or lacy Spencerian script, using a silver or gold marker. Or, enter lines from poems on each card. For a very formal meal, consider propping up a menu at each place setting with a little vase of flowers.

If your meal is too casual for formal place cards, there are other fun, clever ways to personalize the table. The Victorians, in their affection for novelty and surprise, also loved to highlight each place setting with a little gift. The gift could range from a simple flower on each plate, to a small bouquet, to a modest present.

Invitations to a Victorian dinner were always sent by handwritten letter. Perhaps you could invite your guests to come in period dress—lacy dresses and trimmed blouses, fans and gloves—for a special soirée. Ask one of your more talented guests to sing or perform on their instrument of choice, as was customary then. The music could range from classical Victorian composers, like Chopin or Brahms, to Gilbert and Sullivan.

"The art of dining well is no slight art, the pleasure not a slight pleasure."

MICHEL DE MONTAIGNE

A VICTORIAN BREAKFAST

Unlike continental Europe, where a roll and coffee were the only morning sustenance, the nineteenth-century British breakfast was a bountiful affair. The sideboard was generously set with an array of chafing dishes containing porridge, scrambled eggs, rashers of bacon (thick and more like Canadian bacon), sausages, cold smoked meats, meat pies, kippers (herrings cold-smoked in brine), deviled kidneys, broiled fish, grilled tomatoes and mushrooms, toast, rolls, several kinds of jams, stewed fruit, and coffee or tea. Waffles were then considered a dessert course.

Porridge, a Scottish invention, was the standard Victorian breakfast dish of middle-class Britain. (Dried and toasted cereals were not invented until the 1920's.) Often served as a first course, like soup, porridge was usually eaten with cream and sugar. But as Jessup Whitehead's 1893 *Stewards Handbook* listed no less than twenty-eight different kinds of porridge, some extra creative toppings would certainly not be un-Victorian-like.

Across the Atlantic—especially among the wealthy Victorians of New York—it was fashionable to rise late and have a *déjeuner à la fourchette*, or "fork breakfast," which was actually a substantial midday luncheon. Less avid about meat pies and kippers, the Americans had their own

hearty breakfast favorites, including muffins, waffles and pancakes.

On weekends, when there is time to linger over breakfast, it is worthwhile recovering some of these old-fashioned dishes. As it was the custom then to serve oneself directly from the sideboard, a breakfast buffet would spare the host or hostess extra serving work and still be in the proper Victorian spirit.

"Bring porridge, bring sausage, bring fish for a start, bring kidneys and mushrooms and partridges' legs, but let the foundation be bacon and eggs."

A. P. HERBERT

MENU

Porridge
Eggs à la Victoria
Grilled Tomatoes
Fresh Fruit
Coffee or English Breakfast Tea

Porridge

2 cups (16 fl. oz.) water
½ cup (4 fl. oz.) whole grain oats
2 tbsp. (1½ Br. tbsp.) almonds, chopped
1 tbsp. (¾ Br. tbsp.) light brown sugar
¼ cup (2 fl. oz.) light cream

In a medium saucepan, bring water to a boil. Add the oats and cook over medium heat, stirring until thickened, about 5 minutes. Reduce heat and simmer uncovered 20 to 30 minutes, stirring occasionally until oats are cooked. Remove from heat. Stir in the almonds and brown sugar, then add the cream. (Other suggested toppings: fresh berries, peaches, cooked apples, raisins, butter, or maple syrup) Serves 2.

Eggs à la Victoria

6 tbsp. (4½ Br. tbsp.) butter
1½ tsp. (1 Br. tsp.) curry powder
¾ cup (6 fl. oz.) vegetable stock
2 tbsp. (1½ Br. tbsp.) flour
½ cup (4 fl. oz.) light cream
salt and pepper to taste

4 poached eggs
4 slices Canadian bacon (opt.)
toasted English muffins

In a medium saucepan over medium heat, melt butter. With a whisk or a fork, beat in curry powder, then the vegetable stock. Add flour, stirring well until thickened. Stir in light cream, salt, and pepper. Reduce heat to keep sauce warm while poaching eggs. Place toasted English muffins on individual dishes. Place a slice of bacon on top of each muffin, then a poached egg. Spoon sauce over top. Serves 4.

"Nothing helps scenery like ham and eggs."
MARK TWAIN

A Victorian Country Picnic

With a wealth of unspoiled nature surrounding them, the Victorians found many occasions for picnics, or "frolics," during the golden summer afternoons. Croquet, village green events, horseshoes, regattas, and balloon ascensions were only a few of the many outings that called for a picnic basket. The Fourth of July was, of course, the biggest American picnic event.

Light pastel shades, creams, and whites were de rigueur for a Victorian picnic. A pale-colored cloth or blanket was spread on the grass in the shade, with floral napkins, a bouquet of wildflowers, and a complete set of plates, glasses, and cutlery.

Cool, light foods such as salads, cold or potted meats (today's pâtés) or meat pies, chicken, seafood, ham sandwiches or finger sandwiches, cheese, biscuits, soft summer fruits, ice cream, and elaborately molded gelatin were popular picnic fare.

But there was perhaps no better-loved delicacy at a Victorian picnic than berries. During July and August, many outings were spent picking gooseberries, raspberries, currants, and blueberries. Fresh strawberries—still the tradition at Wimbledon, Ascot, and Henley—were usually served unhulled, with a jug of thick yellow cream for dipping and sugar to sprinkle on top.

Tall summer drinks such as lemonade were very

popular among the American Victorians. Ginger beer and ale were also favorite picnic drinks. Chilled champagne—a traditional dessert accompaniment—still transforms any picnic into an elegant occasion.

To make old-fashioned lemonade: In a large glass pitcher, combine the juice of 6 lemons (8 fl. oz.) with ¾ cup (6 fl. oz.) sugar to taste. Add 4 cups (32 fl. oz.) water, ice cubes, and slices of lemon. Pour into tall glasses garnished with fresh mint.

> *"Seating themselves on the green sward, they eat while the corks fly and there is talk, laughter and merriment, and perfect freedom, for the universe is their drawing room and the sun their lamp. Besides, they have appetite, Nature's special gift, which lends to such a meal a vivacity unknown indoors, however beautiful the surroundings."*

ANTHELME BRILLAT-SAVARIN

MENU

Lobster-Chutney Salad
Vegetable Pasties
Assorted Cheeses
Berries & Cream
Lemonade or Champagne

Lobster-Chutney Salad

Salad

2 cups (16 fl. oz.) cooked lobster, cut into pieces
  (small cooked shrimp may be substituted)
¾ cup (6 fl. oz.) celery, diced
½ cup (4 fl. oz.) shredded coconut

Dressing

½ cup (4 fl. oz.) mayonnaise
½ cup (4 fl. oz.) sour cream
1 tsp. (¾ Br. tsp.) curry powder
1 tsp. (¾ Br. tsp.) lime juice
1 tsp. (¾ Br. tsp.) sugar
1½ tbsp. (1 Br. tbsp.) chutney
salt and pepper as desired

*Mix all ingredients together; chill. Serves 4.
(Optional additions: peanuts, raisins, or grapes)*

*"Good friends, good food, good wine, and good
weather—doth a good picnic make."*

ANONYMOUS

Vegetable Pasties

Dough
¼ cup (2 fl. oz.) warm water
1 (¼-oz.) package active dry yeast
3 cups (24 fl. oz.) all-purpose flour
1 tsp. (¾ Br. tsp.) salt
¾ cup (6 fl. oz.) cool water
1 tbsp. (¾ Br. tbsp.) honey
2 tbsp. (1½ Br. tbsp.) olive oil
2 tbsp. (1½ Br. tbsp.) cornmeal

Filling
1 lb. green cabbage, sliced
1 cup (8 fl. oz.) celery, diced
2 medium leeks, sliced thinly
½ lb. mushrooms, sliced
2 tbsp. (1½ Br. tbsp.) olive oil
½ tsp. salt
¼ tsp. pepper
¼-½ tsp. cayenne pepper, as desired
1 cup (8 fl. oz.) white cheddar or mozzarella cheese,
  finely shredded

Pour warm water into a small bowl. Sprinkle yeast over water and stir until dissolved. In a separate bowl, combine flour and salt. In a glass measuring cup, combine cool water, honey and olive oil. Add honey mixture and dissolved yeast to flour in bowl.

Stir until dough forms. On a floured surface, knead dough until elastic, adding more flour if necessary. Place dough in a large greased bowl. Turn to coat. Cover bowl with a towel and let rise in a warm place for 1 hour or until dough has doubled in bulk.

While dough is rising, heat oil in a large pot over medium heat. Add cabbage, celery, leeks, mushrooms, salt, pepper, and cayenne pepper. Cook 10 minutes, stirring frequently until greens are tender. Let cool. Stir cheese into cooled filling.

Punch dough down. Preheat oven to 450°F. Grease 2 baking sheets and sprinkle them with cornmeal. Divide dough into 8 equal-sized balls. On a lightly floured surface, roll each ball into a thin, flat circle. Place ½ cup (4 fl. oz.) of the vegetable filling on half of each circle. Fold uncovered half of dough over filling to make a half circle. Moisten edges of dough with water and pinch them together. Place on pans and bake for 10 to 12 minutes, or until golden brown. Serve hot or cold. Makes 8 pasties.

"All's well that ends with a good meal."

ARNOLD LOBEL

AFTERNOON TEA

The notion of serving light refreshments with afternoon tea developed in the 1700's when dinner advanced to a later hour. To tide themselves over the gap between meals, those in fashionable society began having tea and little sandwiches around four o'clock. By the Victorian era, it had become the national custom to invite one's friends over for afternoon tea.

"At home" was the Victorian phrase used on invitations to an afternoon tea. From three to six o'clock, members of local society made a round of brief calls upon those acquaintances who were "at home." The hostess usually sat behind an ornate tea service—silver or china—and

poured the brew into delicate, nearly transparent tea cups. The tea table was set with a lace cloth, plates, spoons, butter knives, and dainty white napkins.

Afternoon tea usually included thinly sliced bread and butter (or cucumber sandwiches in the summer), or crumpets, or scones, preserves, cake, and, of course, a pot of tea. More formal teas were usually held when a prominent person was being honored by the community or a new bride was entertaining for the first time. At these receptions the table would be filled with a variety of tea sandwiches, biscuits, breads, preserves, and several types of cakes displayed on tiered cake stands. Sometimes a glass of sherry or Madeira would be offered. As it was not meant to be a meal in itself, the food was always light and dainty.

Traditionally, the oolong and more delicate black teas are favored with the lighter afternoon fare. Among the best afternoon teas are Darjeeling, Earl Grey, Ceylon, Jasmine, Formosa Oolong, Orange Pekoe, and Yunnan.

To make a perfect pot of tea: Begin with fine quality, fresh tea leaves and fresh, cold water. Use a ceramic teapot (which best retains heat and flavor), and warm the pot first by rinsing it with hot water. Measure one heaping teaspoon of tea (or one tea bag) per cup plus one for the pot. When the water has reached the just-boiling point, pour it immediately into the teapot. Cover and let brew for three to five minutes—no longer—before pouring the tea. If the tea leaves are loose, strain them through a tea infuser. Then remove the tea leaves or bags from the brewed tea to keep it from getting bitter. Offer milk, sugar, honey or lemon slices to accompany the tea.

To make tea sandwiches: The bread should be untextured, firm, and very thinly sliced. Spreading the bread with softened butter, cream cheese, or herbed mayonnaise will keep it moist and also prevent sogginess. Remove the crusts after the sandwiches have been spread, then cut them into desired shapes. Besides the traditional cucumber, watercress or pâté toppings, some modern-day garnishes might include tomato and basil, avocado and watercress, or asparagus tips on lemon mayonnaise.

Afternoon tea is a tradition in entertaining we would do well to revive. The soothing ritual allows us to refresh ourselves and our friends with a bit of momentary pleasure. Although elaborate tea services are rarely used now, the enjoyment of the ritual is still enhanced by a lovely presentation with pretty linens, fine cups, and a small bouquet of flowers.

"A tea table without a big cake in the country in England would look very bare and penurious. The ideal table should include some sort of hot buttered toast or scone, one or two sorts of sandwiches, a plate of small light cakes and our friend the luncheon cake. Add a pot of jam or honey, and a plate of brown and white bread and butter...and every eye will sparkle..."

LADY SYSONBY

MENU

Tea Sandwiches
Crumpets
Butter & Preserves
Victoria Sponge Cake
Tea or Sherry

Crumpets

1 (¼-oz.) package active dry yeast
2 tsp. (1½ Br. tsp.) sugar
1 cup (8 fl. oz.) warm water
2 cups (16 fl. oz.) all-purpose flour
½ tsp. salt
1 cup (8 fl. oz.) warm milk

In a measuring cup, dissolve yeast and sugar in warm water. In a large bowl, combine flour and salt. Make a well in the center and pour in yeast mixture; stir well. Cover with plastic wrap and let stand in a warm place for 1 hour or until batter has doubled in bulk. Add warm milk to batter, stirring vigorously until well mixed and somewhat runny.

On a greased griddle or heavy skillet over medium heat, place several greased crumpet rings, poached egg rings, or cookie rings. Pour the batter up to ½ inch into each ring. Cook until underside is browned and top is firm and surfaced with holes. (If no holes appear, add more water to the batter.) Carefully remove rings. Turn crumpets and cook a few minutes longer, until lightly browned. Grease rings again and repeat with another batch. Makes about 12 crumpets.

When ready to eat, toast the crumpets and serve with butter and preserves.

Victoria Sponge Cake

Cake

5 oz. butter, softened
⅔ cup (5⅓ fl. oz.) sugar
3 eggs
1¼ cups (10 fl. oz.) all-purpose flour

Filling

4 oz. butter, softened
¾ cup (6 fl. oz.) powdered (icing) sugar
1 tbsp. (¾ fl. oz.) milk
½ tsp. vanilla extract
4 tbsp. (3 Br. tbsp.) cherry preserves

Preheat oven to 350°F. Grease two 7-inch cake pans. In a mixing bowl, cream together butter and sugar. Add eggs one at a time, beating well. Mix in the flour. Divide batter evenly into cake pans. Bake 15 to 20 minutes until golden in color. Remove from heat. Let cool in pans 10 minutes, then turn out onto wire racks.

In a medium bowl, cream together butter and powdered sugar. Add milk to make a creamy consistency. Then add the vanilla.

To assemble, spread butter cream on one cake layer. Carefully spread preserves on top of butter cream. Add second cake layer. Dust top with additional powdered sugar.

HIGH TEA

It is a widely held assumption that high tea is a more elaborate version of low tea, or afternoon tea. In Victorian times, however, high tea was the evening meal for the working classes.

Although the middle and upper Victorian classes ate their main meal in the evening, the working population still had theirs in the middle of the day. Then, at six o'clock, the family sat down to a modest supper with a simple hot dish, bread and butter, and a cake or tarts. On weekends and holidays, guests were often invited. Although accompanied by pints of strong tea (or ale, more likely), the assembly of hearty foods made it distinctly different from the delicate fare of afternoon tea. Delightfully informal, the ritual of high tea is still common in many parts of England.

Some favorite supper dishes of the period included hearty soups, Welsh Rarebit (creamy toasted cheese), meat pies and Cornish pasties, Scotch eggs, mushrooms on toast, and fish and chips.

As it was customary to buy and roast a large joint of meat once a week, the supper dishes also depended on a family's ingenuity in using up the leftovers. A familiar saying was: "Hot on Sunday, cold on Monday, hashed on Tuesday, minced on Wednesday, curried on Thursday,

broth on Friday, cottage pie Saturday."

Meat pies—the mainstay of the Victorian supper and a hearty sustainer on chilly days—date back to medieval times when they were highly spiced with peppery meats and hidden under a pastry crust. By the nineteenth century, the crust was usually replaced by potatoes. Fillings varied from region to region. Fidget Pie, Star-Gazy Pie, Pork and Potato Pie, Steak and Kidney Pie, and Shepherd's Pie were among the favorites.

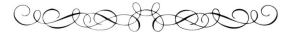

"Things taste better in small houses."
QUEEN VICTORIA

MENU

Mulligatawny Soup
Shepherd's Pie
Crusty Bread
Pears with Cheddar Cheese
Tea or Ale

Mulligatawny Soup

1 lb. boneless skinless chicken breasts
3 tbsp. (2¼ Br. tbsp.) all-purpose flour
3 tbsp. (2¼ Br. tbsp.) butter
1½ cups (12 fl. oz.) onions, chopped
2 cups (16 fl. oz.) carrots, chopped
2 cups (16 fl. oz.) celery, chopped
2 cups (16 fl. oz.) green apples, peeled, cored and chopped
1½ tbsp. (1 Br. tbsp.) curry powder
3 tsp. (2¼ Br. tsp.) salt
½ tsp. pepper
¼ tsp. chili powder
⅓ cup (2⅔ fl. oz.) shredded coconut
apple juice, as desired
half and half, as desired

Wash chicken breasts and pat dry. Roll in flour and set remaining flour aside. In large stock pot, melt butter over medium-high heat. Brown chicken on all sides; then remove breasts and set aside. Add the chopped onions, carrots, celery, apples and reserved flour to the stock pot. Cook for 5 minutes, stirring frequently. Then stir in curry, salt, pepper, chili powder, coconut, chicken, and 6 cups (48 fl. oz.) water. Bring to a boil; reduce heat and simmer covered for 1½ hours. Remove from heat and let cool for 10 minutes. Place stock pot in refrigerator overnight.

The next day, skim off top layer of fat. Remove

chicken breasts, cut into pieces and return to stock pot. While reheating soup, thin it out by adding apple juice and half and half to desired color and consistency. Makes 6 to 8 servings.

(Note: In Victorian times, Mulligatawny Soup was usually strained into a consommé and served as a first course to dinner. If left as is, however, this spicy Indian soup makes a substantial supper dish.)

Shepherd's Pie

3 tbsp. (2¼ Br. tbsp.) oil
2 medium onions, finely chopped
2 garlic cloves, minced
1½ lbs. ground beef
½ lb. mushrooms, sliced
1 6-oz. can tomato paste
1 tbsp. (¾ Br. tbsp.) all-purpose flour
½ tsp. crushed rosemary
½ cup (4 fl. oz.) wine
½ cup (4 fl. oz.) water
salt and pepper to taste
6 medium potatoes, peeled
6 tbsp. (4½ Br. tbsp.) butter
1 cup (8 fl. oz.) milk
paprika for garnish

In a large stock pot, cover potatoes with water and boil gently until tender. While potatoes are cooking, heat oil in a large skillet over medium heat. Add onions and garlic; cook until soft. Add the ground beef; cook until browned and drain off any fat. Add the mushrooms, cooking briefly. Then stir in the tomato paste, flour, rosemary, salt, pepper, wine and water. Simmer for 15 minutes.

When potatoes are done, remove from heat and drain. Preheat oven to 350°F. Mash potatoes briefly, then whip in butter, milk, salt, and pepper. When meat mixture is done, line up 6 individual well-greased ovenproof bowls (or 1 large casserole dish). Spread meat mixture at the bottom of each bowl, followed by the mashed potatoes on top. Sprinkle paprika over the potatoes and bake uncovered for 30 minutes or until very lightly browned. Serves 6.

*"If beef's the King of Meat,
potato's the Queen of the Garden World."*
IRISH SAYING

A VICTORIAN DINNER

For a Victorian, an invitation to dinner was the highest social compliment and table rituals were at their most elaborate. It was and still is an occasion to dress up and use one's best china, glasses and linens.

The proper way to begin a Victorian dinner was with one or more types of soups, accompanied by an aperitif such as sherry. A good soup—an aperitif in itself—was meant to sharpen the appetite, yet dull the hunger. Turtle soup, mulligatawny soup (served as a consommé), lobster bisque, almond soup, and watercress soup were among the favorite soups of the day. Watercress grew abundantly along the streams and was used widely by Victorian cooks.

The second course included a fish dish or two, along with white wine. Then came the roasted meats such as beef, mutton and pork, plus a variety of cream sauces. The fourth course was a mixed medley of fowl and game dishes, relishes and aspics, and that obligatory part of any Victorian dinner—pudding.

At this point the crumbs were swept up and finger bowls were put before each guest. Then the desserts were placed on the table all at one time. Desserts often featured ices, fruit (usually dusted with sugar), and the much-loved Victorian creams and jellies, custards and sweet concoc-

tions such as flummery, syllabub and trifle. Finally, individual wedges of cheese, such as ripe Stilton, were passed around on an elegant plate, accompanied by port or Madeira—the ceremonial end to the meal.

A word about pudding: Pudding was originally a number of savory ingredients boiled in a bag. By the nineteenth century, the pudding was more often sweet and steamed in a suet crust. Eventually it became an indefinite term that encompassed pies, tarts, charlottes, creams, trifle, blancmanges, and gelatin; sweet or savory; steamed, boiled, or baked; and with or without a lining. Isabella Beeton felt the subject important enough to provide her readers with over 200 pudding recipes. Among them were such colorful names as Sussex Pond Pudding and Spotted Dick (a simple steamed pudding with raisins and currants). Even the American pumpkin pie developed from English Harvest Home Pudding. Yorkshire Pudding—a traditional accompaniment to beef—is the only savory pudding made today.

Although plain roast meats were then the focal point of the meal, nowadays we might dispense with the meat course altogether. A modern version of a Victorian dinner might well feature the lighter, healthier Victorian favorites such as seafood, vegetables, potatoes, and very light sauces...with perhaps a rich, decadent dessert thrown in, for tradition's sake only, of course!

MENU

Sherry
Watercress Soup
Poached Salmon with Dijon Sauce
Rosemary Roasted Potatoes
Peas with Mint
Almond Charlotte Russe
French White Wine

Watercress Soup

3 cups (24 fl. oz.)
watercress leaves, chopped

2 tbsp. (1½ Br. tbsp.)
shallots, chopped

4 tbsp. (3 Br. tbsp.) butter

2 tbsp. (1½ Br. tbsp.) all-
purpose flour

3 cups (24 fl. oz.) chicken
stock

½ cup (4 fl. oz.) white wine

1 tbsp. (¾ Br. tbsp.) lemon
juice

1 cup (8 fl. oz.) cream

salt and pepper

sour cream for garnish (opt.)

*Wash watercress leaves well. In a medium sauce-
pan, sauté watercress and shallots in butter until
limp. Stir in flour; then add chicken stock, wine and
lemon juice. Cook on medium heat for 10 minutes,
stirring occasionally. Remove from heat and purée
soup in a blender or food processor. Return soup to
saucepan and add cream. Season with salt and
pepper. Heat just to boiling. If desired, garnish each
bowl of soup with a dollop of sour cream swirled with
a toothpick, and sprinkle watercress leaves on top.
Can serve hot or cold. Serves 4 to 6.*

*"Of all the items on the menu,
soup is that which exacts the most delicate
perfection and the strictest attention."*

Auguste Escoffier

Poached Salmon with Dijon Sauce

Poached Salmon

1 cup (8 fl. oz.) dry white wine
½ cup (4 fl. oz.) celery, chopped
¼ cup (2 fl. oz.) carrots, chopped
1 bay leaf
1 tsp. (¾ Br. tsp.) salt
¼ tsp. peppercorns
1 tbsp. (¾ Br. tbsp.) lemon juice
4-6 salmon filets

In a poaching pan or a large pan with a rack, pour in 2 quarts of water. Add all ingredients except salmon. Bring to a boil. Put rack in place. Reduce heat, then add salmon filets. Cover and simmer 10 minutes until fish is just cooked. Drain and refrigerate. Serve cold with Dijon sauce.

*"After a good dinner,
one can forgive anybody,
even one's own relations."*

OSCAR WILDE

Dijon Sauce

2 egg yolks
¼ cup (2 fl. oz.) virgin olive oil
2 tsp. (1½ Br. tsp.) vinegar
4 tsp. (3 Br. tsp.) prepared Dijon mustard
2 tbsp. (1½ Br. tbsp.) whipping cream
½ tsp. sugar
salt and pepper to taste
1 tbsp. (¾ Br. tbsp.) capers, drained
1 tbsp. (¾ Br. tbsp.) fresh dill, chopped

In a medium bowl, with an electric mixer on medium speed, beat egg yolks until thick. Very slowly add olive oil, one teaspoon at a time, beating until thick. Beat in vinegar, then add mustard, whipping cream, sugar, salt and pepper; continue beating. Add capers and dill and beat 30 seconds more. Refrigerate.

"Fish is held out to be one of the greatest luxuries of the table and not only necessary, but even indispensable at all dinners where there is any pretense to excellence or fashion."

MRS. ISABELLA BEETON

Rosemary Roasted Potatoes

small red potatoes
olive oil
salt and pepper
sprigs of fresh rosemary

Preheat oven to 350°F. Cut potatoes in half. Brush both sides with olive oil. Season with salt and pepper. Place cut sides down in a foil-lined baking pan. Place sprigs of rosemary on top. Cook for 10 minutes. Turn potatoes over, with rosemary sprigs on top. Cook 20 to 30 minutes more until done. Remove rosemary. Turn on broiler and cook an additional 3 to 5 minutes if desired.

*"If you intend to decline an invitation to dinner,
do so at as early a date as possible.
A dinner invitation, once accepted,
is a sacred obligation.
If you die before the dinner takes place,
your executor must attend the dinner."*

WARD MCALLISTER

Almond Charlotte Russe

18 ladyfingers
⅓ cup (2⅔ fl. oz.) sherry
3 tbsp. (2¼ Br. tbsp.) water
1 envelope unflavored gelatin
⅓ cup (2⅔ fl. oz.) sugar
½ cup (4 fl. oz.) milk
1 tsp. (¾ Br. tsp.) almond extract
1½ cups (12 fl. oz.) heavy whipping cream
½ cup (4 fl. oz.) slivered almonds
fresh raspberries

Mix sherry with water and drizzle over lady-fingers. Place ladyfingers in a 6½" charlotte mold or other suitable mold.

In a saucepan over medium heat, dissolve gelatin and sugar in milk using a whisk until well mixed. Bring to a gentle boil and continue to cook 2 minutes more, stirring constantly. Stir in the almond extract. Chill mixture. Meanwhile, beat the whipping cream with an electric mixer until stiff. When gelatin mixture has just started to set, approximately 10 minutes, beat with a whisk until fluffy. Beat ¼ of the cream into the gelatin mixture until blended. Fold in the rest of the cream, then the almonds. Spoon the cream mixture into the mold. Chill for several hours.

Unmold the charlotte onto serving plate. Top with fresh raspberries. Garnish with additional whipped cream and raspberries if desired.

"The pleasure in giving a dinner is mostly the pleasure of giving yourself. The effort you take is your way of showing your company that you care about them enough to give them a good time."

MARGUERITE KELLY & ELIA PARSONS

GRAPHIC DESIGN BY GRETCHEN GOLDIE

PHOTO STYLING BY SUE TALLON

ACKNOWLEDGMENTS

RUTH HANKS, JEAN HYDE, DEBORAH JOYCE, SUSAN MALJAN,
JOE POSHEK, CHRISTOPHER AND MELONIE TALLON,
AND JULIETTE TRYGG